O CONVEYS BLACKACRE TO A FOR LIFE:
A PRESENT ESTATES & FUTURE INTERESTS STUDY GUIDE

Tanya D. Marsh

Copyright © 2019 God's Acre Publishing

All rights reserved.

ISBN: 9781798037546

CONTENTS

1	Introduction to Present Estates and Future Interests	1
2	Fee Simple Absolute	5
3	Life Estate	7
4	Fee Tail	10
5	Term of Years	12
6	Fee Simple Determinable	14
7	Fee Simple Subject to Condition Subsequent	16
8	Fee Simple Subject to Executory Limitation	18
9	The Difference Between FSD and FSSCS	20
10	Remainders	28
11	Problem Set Instructions	33
12	Problem Set I: Finite Estates	34
13	Problem Set II: Defeasible Estates	39
14	Problem Set III: Remainders	43
15	Problem Set IV: Review	48
16	Problem Set I: Answers for Present Estates	52
17	Problem Set I: Complete Answers	55
18	Problem Set II: Answers for Present Estates	59
19	Problem Set II: Complete Answers	61
20	Problem Set III: Complete Answers	64
21	Problem Set IV: Complete Answers	68

CHAPTER 1

INTRODUCTION TO PRESENT ESTATES & FUTURE INTERESTS

This book is not intended to comprehensively teach the intricate rules of Present Estates and Future Interests. Instead, it is designed as a supplement for students currently studying the subject, or as a refresher for graduates studying for the bar exam. Present Estates and Future Interests have a long, complicated history in English and U.S. law, and a number of different names for the same Estate have been used by courts and treatise writers. This book uses the most common modern terms, which are consistent with the terms used most commonly for bar exam preparation.

1. **Definition of Estate**

The Restatement (First) of Property §9 defines the word "Estate."

> The word "estate," as it is used in this Restatement, means an interest in land which:
> (a) Is or may become possessory; and
> (b) Is ownership measured in terms of duration.

There are two main divisions of Estates: (i) Present Estates and (ii) Future Interests.

- A **Present Estate** is the present ownership of a present possessory interest in real property.

- A **Future Interest** is the present ownership of: (i) a right to future possession; or (ii) the potential right to future possession of real property.

2. **Three Categories of Present Estates**

There are three categories of Present Estates:

- Fee Simple Absolute
- Finite Estates
- Fee Simples Defeasible

The **Fee Simple Absolute** is the largest present estate that may be created. It is of indefinite duration.

The three **Finite Estates** are of a limited duration. We may not know when they will end, but we know that they are certain to end. They are different from the Fee Simple Absolute, which is of an unlimited duration, and the **Fee Simples Defeasible**, which may be of an unlimited duration or may end.

3. **Seven Types of Present Estates**

The three categories of Present Estates may be broken down into seven different types:

- Fee Simple Absolute
- Finite Estates
    - Life Estate
    - Fee Tail
    - Term of Years
- Defeasible Fees (also known as Fee Simples Defeasible)
    - Fee Simple Determinable (FSD)
    - Fee Simple Subject to Condition Subsequent (FSSCS)
    - Fee Simple Subject to Executory Limitation (FSSEL)

Each of the seven types of Present Estates are described in detail in Chapters 2 through 9.

4. **Five Categories of Future Interests**

There are five categories of Future Interests. Three categories which may be held by the original grantor, and two categories which may be held by a person other than the original grantor.

Future Interests held by the original grantor:

- Reversion
- Possibility of Reverter
- Right of Entry (also known as a Power to Terminate)

Future Interests held by a person other than the original grantor:

- Remainder
- Executory Interest

5. **Nine Types of Future Interests.**

Each of the categories of Future Interests held by the original grantor include only one type of future interest. The two categories of Future Interests held by a person other than the grantor contain six different types of Future Interest, for a total of nine different types of Future Interest.

- Reversion
- Possibility of Reverter
- Right of Entry (also known as a Power to Terminate)

- Remainder
  - Indefeasibly Vested Remainder
  - Vested Remainder Subject to Divestment
  - Vested Remainder Subject to Open
  - Contingent Remainder
- Executory Interest
  - Shifting Executory Interest
  - Springing Executory Interest

6. Methods of Transferring/Creating Present Estates and Future Interests

In general, Present Estates and Future Interests may be transferred via conveyance, testamentary transfer, or intestate succession. Some special restrictions on transfer do apply to certain types of Estates.

Transfer by Conveyance. A person may make an *inter vivos* transfer of an Estate by gift or sale (sometimes called a "grant"). If an Estate may be transferred by conveyance it is referred to as "**alienable.**"

- All seven Present Estates are alienable.
- Historically, Reversions and Vested Remainders were the only types of Future Interests that were fully alienable. Contingent Remainders and Executory Interests were not alienable because they were considered to be too speculative. Most states now permit the alienation of Contingent Remainders and Executory Interests although a few restrict their *inter vivos* transfer. Historically, Possibilities of Reverter and Rights of Entry were similarly non-alienable. Today, the states are divided with respect to their alienation.

Testamentary Transfer. A person may transfer an Estate via a testamentary gift contained in a will. If an Estate may be transferred by will it is referred to as "**devisable.**"

- Five Present Estates are devisable; only Life Estates and Fee Tails may not be transferred via testamentary gift.
- Most Future Interests are devisable, however, states on split on the question of whether Possibilities of Reverter and Rights of Entry may be devised.

Intestate Succession. An Estate owned by a person at death and not devised via a will may be transferred via the laws of intestate succession to an heir or heirs. If an Estate may be transferred by intestate succession it is referred to as "**inheritable**" or "**descendible.**"

- Six Present Estates are descendible. Only the Life Estate is not descendible.
- All Future Interests may descend except in South Carolina—in that state neither the Possibility of Reverter nor the Right of Entry may pass by intestate succession.

O CONVEYS BLACKACRE TO A FOR LIFE

Type of Present Estate	Alienable?	Devisable?	Descendible?
Fee Simple Absolute	Yes	Yes	Yes
Life Estate	Yes	No	No
Fee Tail	Yes	No	Yes
Term of Years	Yes	Yes	Yes
Fee Simple Determinable	Yes	Yes	Yes
Fee Simple Subject to Condition Subsequent	Yes	Yes	Yes
Fee Simple Subject to Executory Limitation	Yes	Yes	Yes

Type of Future Interest	Alienable?	Devisable?	Descendible?
Reversion	Yes	Yes	Yes
Possibility of Reverter	States divided	States divided	Yes, except SC
Right of Entry	States divided	States divided	Yes, except SC
Indefeasibly Vested Remainder	Yes	Yes	Yes
Vested Remainder Subject to Divestment	Yes	Yes	Yes
Vested Remainder Subject to Open	Yes	Yes	Yes
Contingent Remainder	Majority rule	Yes	Yes
Shifting Executory Interest	Majority rule	Yes	Yes
Springing Executory Interest	Majority rule	Yes	Yes

CHAPTER 2
FEE SIMPLE ABSOLUTE

1. Definition

The Restatement (First) of Property §15 defines a "**Fee Simple Absolute**."

> An estate in fee simple absolute is an estate in fee simple which is not subject to a special limitation or a condition subsequent or an executory limitation.

2. Words of Limitation

The words of limitation necessary to create a Fee Simple Absolute are "and his/her heirs" or, if dealing with legal entities like a corporation, "and its successors and assigns." Historically, the words of limitation "to A" were deemed to create a Life Estate but at modern law, a transfer "to A" creates a Fee Simple Absolute.

3. Future Interest

No future interest follows a Fee Simple Absolute.

4. Example Problems

Example 1

O conveys Blackacre to A and his heirs.

A has a Fee Simple Absolute.

Example 2

O conveys Blackacre to A and his heirs. A has two children at the time of the conveyance, X and Y.

A has a Fee Simple Absolute.

The fact that A has two children is irrelevant. The words "and his heirs" are not words of purchase, identifying the owner of the present estate, they are words of limitation, defining the estate. By the way, X and Y aren't even A's heirs—no one has heirs until they die and the laws of intestate succession are employed to identify heirs.

Example 3

O conveys Blackacre to A.

> *A has a Fee Simple Absolute*

The Fee Simple Absolute is the default estate. If an instrument is ambiguous regarding whether a Fee Simple Absolute or a lesser present estate was intended to be created, rules of construction typically instruct courts to construe in favor of a Fee Simple Absolute. An instrument will only create a lesser present estate if it expressly and unambiguously does so.

Example 4

O conveys Blackacre to Zeeke. (Zeeke is a dog.)

> *O has a Fee Simple Absolute.*

Conveyances to non-human animals are invalid.

Example 5

O conveys Blackacre to ABC Corporation, Inc., and its successors and assigns.

> *A has a Fee Simple Absolute*

Conveyances to legal entities such as corporations are perfectly fine.

CHAPTER 3
LIFE ESTATE

1. Definition

The Restatement (First) of Property §18 defines a "**Life Estate**."

> An estate for life is an estate which is not an estate of inheritance, and
> (a) is an estate which is specifically described as to duration in terms of the life or lives of one or more human beings, and is not terminable at any fixed or computable period of time; or
> (b) though not so specifically described as is required under the rule stated in Clause (a), is an estate which cannot last longer than the life or live of one or more human beings, and is not terminable at any fixed or computable period of time or at the will of the transferor.

2. Words of Limitation

The words of limitation necessary to create a Life Estate are:

- "for life"
- "until ___ dies"
- "so long as _____ is alive"
- "during the term of his life"
- "for his use and benefit for the remainder of his life"

3. Future Interest

If the future interest following a Life Estate is held by the original grantor, it is called a **Reversion**.

If the future interest following a Life Estate is held by anyone other than the original grantor, it is called a **Remainder**. There are four kinds of Remainders. See Chapter 10.

Reversions are freely alienable, devisable, and descendible. Vested remainders are freely alienable, devisable, and descendible. States differ with respect to the alienability of contingent remainders.

4. Example Problems

Example 1

O conveys Blackacre to A for life.

> *A has a Life Estate.*
>
> *O has a Reversion in Fee Simple Absolute.*

A both owns the Life Estate and is the "measuring life"—upon A's death the Life Estate will automatically terminate.

Example 2

O devises Blackacre to A until A dies, then to B and his heirs.

> *A has a Life Estate.*
>
> *B has an Indefeasibly Vested Remainder in Fee Simple Absolute.*

Example 3

O conveys Blackacre to A so long as A is alive, then to B.

> *A has a Life Estate.*
>
> *B has an Indefeasibly Vested Remainder in Fee Simple Absolute.*

Note that a Life Estate can be created in favor of one person and defined by the life of another. This type of Life Estate is called "**Life Estate *pur autre vie*.**"

Example 4

O conveys Blackacre to A so long as B remains alive.

> *A has a Life Estate pur autre vie (for the life of B).*
>
> *O has a Reversion in Fee Simple Absolute.*
>
> *B has nothing.*

In Example 4, B is the measuring life even though B has no interest in Blackacre. Note that while a legal entity like a corporation may own a Life Estate, it may not serve as the measuring life. Note also that non-humans may not own any property interest and attempted transfers to non-humans are void.

Example 5

O devises Blackacre to her pet cat Raspberry for the remainder of her life.

O's Estate has a Fee Simple Absolute because the attempted devise fails.

Example 6

O conveys Blackacre to ABC Corporation, Inc. for life.

O has a Fee Simple Absolute

This conveyance failed because a corporation cannot be the measuring life for a Life Estate.

Example 7

O conveys Blackacre to ABC Corporation, Inc. for the life of A.

ABC Corporation, Inc. has a Life Estate pur autre vie (for the life of A).

O has a Reversion in Fee Simple Absolute.

A has nothing.

Unlike Example 6, Example 7 creates a Life Estate in ABC Corporation, Inc. because a human is used as the measuring life.

Example 8

O conveys Blackacre to A for life. A then conveys its Present Estate to ABC Corporation, Inc.

ABC Corporation, Inc. has a Life Estate pur autre vie (for the life of A).

O has a Reversion in Fee Simple Absolute.

A has nothing.

Example 9

O conveys Blackacre "to B, but O reserves to herself the exclusive possession, use and enjoyment of Blackacre during the remainder of O's life."

O has a Life Estate

B has an Indefeasibly Vested Remainder in Fee Simple Absolute

CHAPTER 4

FEE TAIL

1. Definition

The Restatement (First) of Property §17 defines a "**Fee Tail**" as "an estate of potentially infinite duration inheritable only by issue of the first taker." In other words, a Fee Tail is an Estate which is specifically described as to duration in terms of the lives of a human being and that human being's descendants.

A subset of the Fee Tail is the **Fee Tail Male**, in which property passes by descent from the patriarch of the family to the next closest male relative. For example, the fact that Longbourn was "entailed" in a Fee Tail Male was the primary problem facing the Bennet family in Jane Austen's *Pride and Prejudice*. Because Mr. Bennet had no sons, upon his death the family home would descend to his paternal cousin Mr. Collins. The Fee Tail Male was also the primary problem facing the Crawley family in *Downton Abbey*.

2. Words of Limitation

The words of limitation necessary to create a Fee Tail are:

- "and the heirs of his/her body"

3. Future Interest

If the future interest following a Fee Tail is held by the original grantor, it is called a **Reversion**.

If the future interest following a Fee Tail is held by anyone other than the original grantor, it is called a **Remainder**. There are four kinds of Remainders. See Chapter 10.

4. Example Problems

<u>Example 1</u>

O conveys Blackacre to A and the heirs of his body.

A has a Fee Tail.

O has a Reversion in Fee Simple Absolute.

Example 2

O devises Blackacre to A and the heirs of her body, then to B.

A has a Fee Tail.

B has an Indefeasibly Vested Remainder in Fee Simple Absolute.

Example 3

O devises Blackacre to C and her children.

C and her children share Blackacre as tenants in common.

The language "and her children" will not be interpreted to create a Fee Tail because it is missing the "magic" words of limitation "and the heirs of her body."

Note that although they are a popular plot device in English literature, in most states, Fee Tails are prohibited by statutory law. The states differ in terms of their treatment of Fee Tails. Some states convert them into a Fee Simple Absolute in the original transferee. Some convert them into a Life Estate in the original transferee, with the Remainder in Fee Simple Absolute to the original transferee's heirs. Four states (Delaware, Maine, Massachusetts, and Rhode Island) still recognize the Fee Tail. In these states, the holder of the Fee Tail can convert the estate to a Fee Simple Absolute through an inter vivos transfer called disentailing. A Fee Tail is not devisable or descendible.

CHAPTER 5
TERM OF YEARS

1. Definition

The Restatement (First) of Property §19 defines a "**Term of Years.**"

> An estate for years is an estate, the duration of which is fixed in units of a year or multiples or divisions thereof.

A Term of Years is the only one of the Present Estates referred to as a "non-freehold estate." The distinction between freehold and non-freehold estates was historically important, but there is essentially no difference under modern U.S. law.

2. Words of Limitation

The words of limitation necessary to create a Term of Years are:

- "for [period of time]"

3. Future Interest

If the future interest following a Term of Years is held by the original grantor, it is called a **Reversion**.

If the future interest following a Term of Years is held by anyone other than the original grantor, it is called a **Remainder**. There are four kinds of Remainders. See Chapter 10.

4. Example Problems

Example 1

O devises Blackacre to A for one month, then to B.

A has a Term of Years.

B has an Indefeasibly Vested Remainder in Fee Simple Absolute.

Example 2

O conveys Blackacre to A for 10 years.

A has a Term of Years.

O has a Reversion in Fee Simple Absolute.

Example 3

O conveys Blackacre to A for three weeks from January 1 of next year.

A has a Term of Years.

O has a Reversion in Fee Simple Absolute.

Example 4

O conveys Blackacre to A for 200 years.

In most jurisdictions, *A has a Term of Years and O has a Reversion in Fee Simple Absolute.* In some jurisdictions, a lengthy Term of Years will automatically convert to a Life Estate with O retaining a Reversion in Fee Simple Absolute.

CHAPTER 6

FEE SIMPLE DETERMINABLE (FSD)

1. Definition

A **Fee Simple Determinable** (FSD) includes words that define the period of time that the property will be held by the grantee based on a special limitation. In other words, a Fee Simple Determinable may last forever, or it may automatically expire upon the occurrence of a stated event or the lapse of a required condition.

Historically, the Fee Simple Determinable was defined as a Fee Simple with a "special limitation." The Restatement (First) of Property §23 explains that the "term 'special limitation' denotes that part of the language of a conveyance which causes the created interest automatically to expire upon the occurrence of a stated event, and thus provides for a terminability in addition to that normally characteristic of such interest."

2. Words of Limitation

The classic words of limitation necessary to create a Fee Simple Determinable are:

- "as long as"
- "so long as"
- "until"
- "during"
- "while"

3. Future Interest

A **Possibility of Reverter** always follows a Fee Simple Determinable and is always held by the original grantor. A Possibility of Reverter automatically becomes possessory when the condition subsequent is triggered.

4. Example Problems

Example 1

O conveys Blackacre to A so long as A does not permit alcohol to be sold at Blackacre.

A has a Fee Simple Determinable.

O has a Possibility of Reverter in Fee Simple Absolute.

Example 2

O conveys Blackacre to A until A is married.

A has a Fee Simple Determinable.

O has a Possibility of Reverter in Fee Simple Absolute.

Example 3

O conveys Blackacre to School District in fee simple as long as Blackacre is used for educational purposes.

School District has a Fee Simple Determinable.

O has a Possibility of Reverter in Fee Simple Absolute.

Example 4

O conveys Blackacre to A for life and thereafter to B and his heirs until A's then oldest living son shall marry.

A has a Life Estate.

B has a Remainder in Fee Simple Determinable.

O has a Possibility of Reverter in Fee Simple Absolute.

A "special limitation" may be combined with any of the Finite Estates. In such cases, the original grantor would have both a Reversion (following the natural expiration of the Finite Estate) and a Possibility of Reverter (if the special limitation is triggered, cutting short the Finite Estate).

Example 5

O conveys Blackacre to A for life or so long as A shall remain childless.

A has a Life Estate Determinable.

O has a Possibility of Reverter in Fee Simple Absolute and a Reversion in Fee Simple Absolute.

CHAPTER 7

FEE SIMPLE SUBJECT TO CONDITION SUBSEQUENT (FSSCS)

1. Definition

A **Fee Simple Subject to Condition Subsequent** (FSSCS) identifies an event which may or may not occur. If the event occurs, the FSSCS shall continue until the original grantor exercises his or her power to terminate the FSSCS. In other words, a Fee Simple Subject to Condition Subsequent may last forever, or it may be cut short if the specified event occurs AND the original grantor takes steps to end the FSSCS. The difference between the Fee Simple Determinable and the Fee Simple Subject to Condition Subsequent is that the FSD ends automatically and the FSSCS requires the original grantor to take action to end it.

The Restatement (First) of Property §24 defines a "condition subsequent" as "that part of the language of a conveyance, by virtue of which upon the occurrence of a stated event the conveyor, or his successor in interest, has the power to terminate the interest which has been created subject to the condition subsequent, but which will continue until the power is exercised."

2. Words of Limitation

The classic words of limitation necessary to create a Fee Simple Subject to Condition Subsequent are:

- "but if"
- "provided"
- "however"
- "on the condition"
- "unless"

If the court determines that the language creating the Defeasible Fee is ambiguous, it will construe in favor of creating a Fee Simple Subject to Condition Subsequent because the automatic forfeiture created by a Fee Simple Determinable is disfavored by the common law.

3. Future Interest

A **Right of Entry** always follows a Fee Simple Subject to Condition Subsequent and is always held by the original grantor. The Right of Entry requires the holder to elect to re-enter the property and reclaim possession after the specified event occurs. It is *not* automatic. Note that the doctrine of laches applies to Rights of Entry and prohibits exercise of a Right of Entry if the holder fails to enforce its right during a reasonable period of time.

4. Example Problems

Example 1

O conveys Blackacre to A, provided that A never permits alcohol to be sold at Blackacre.

A has a Fee Simple Subject to Condition Subsequent.

O has a Right of Entry in Fee Simple Absolute.

Example 2

O conveys Blackacre to A on the condition that A never marries.

A has a Fee Simple Subject to Condition Subsequent.

O has a Right of Entry in Fee Simple Absolute.

Example 3

O conveys Blackacre to A to hold to him and his heirs subject to the condition that if A or his heirs or successors shall during the life of O erect an apartment building on Blackacre, then O may enter and terminate the estate.

A has a Fee Simple Subject to Condition Subsequent.

O has a Right of Entry in Fee Simple Absolute.

Example 4

O conveys Blackacre to A and B and their heirs, but the share hereby conveyed to B is conveyed upon the express condition that if $100 per month is not paid to D during his life by the owners of the share thus conveyed to B, then O may terminate the estate hereby conveyed.

A and B are tenants in common, each with an undivided ½ interest in Blackacre.

A's ½ interest is a Fee Simple Absolute.

B's ½ interest is a Fee Simple Subject to Condition Subsequent.

O has a Right of Entry with respect to B's ½ interest in Blackacre.

CHAPTER 8
FEE SIMPLE SUBJECT TO EXECUTORY LIMITATION (FSSEL)

1. Definition

A **Fee Simple Subject to Executory Limitation** (FSSEL) can be created with language sufficient to create a Fee Simple Determinable (i.e. describing a period of time that ends automatically) or with language sufficient to create a Fee Simple Subject to Condition Subsequent (i.e. describing a trigger that will permit the original grantor to reclaim the property). The FFSEL is different from both the FSD and the FSSCS because with a FSSEL, the Future Interest is always held by a person other than the original grantor.

2. Words of Limitation

The words of limitation necessary to create a Fee Simple Subject to Executory Limitation are:

- "as long as"
- "so long as"
- "until"
- "during"
- "while"
- "but if"
- "provided"
- "however"
- "on the condition"
- "unless"

3. Future Interest

An **Executory Interest** always follows a Fee Simple Subject to Executory Limitation and is always held by a party other than the original grantor. If the language creating the FSSEL is otherwise sufficient to create a Fee Simple Determinable, then the Executory Interest functions like a Possibility of Reverter. If the language creating the FSSEL is otherwise sufficient to create a Fee Simple Subject to Condition Subsequent, then the Executory Interest functions like a Right of Entry.

4. Example Problems

Example 1

O conveys Blackacre to A, provided that A never permits alcohol to be sold at Blackacre, then to B.

A has a Fee Simple Subject to Executory Limitation.

B has a Shifting Executory Interest in Fee Simple Absolute.

Note that there are two different kinds of Executory Interests: Shifting and Springing. **Shifting Executory Interests** follows a FSSEL held by a party other than the original grantor. A **Springing Executory Interest** follows a FSSEL held by the original grantor.

Example 2

O conveys Blackacre to A if and when A marries.

O has a Fee Simple Subject to Executory Limitation.

A has a Springing Executory Interest in Fee Simple Absolute.

Example 3

O devises Blackacre to A so long as A does not permit alcohol to be sold at Blackacre.

A has a Fee Simple Subject to Executory Limitation.

O's Estate has a Shifting Executory Interest in Fee Simple Absolute.

Example 4

O conveys to the Verdon School District on the express condition that Blackacre be used for school purposes and if not, to the Verdon Historical Society.

The Verdon School District has a Fee Simple Subject to Executory Limitation.

The Verdon Historical Society has a Shifting Executory Interest in Fee Simple Absolute.

CHAPTER 9

THE DIFFERENCE BETWEEN FSD AND FSSCS

The Mahrenholz case, decided in Illinois in 1981, provides a thorough discussion of the difference between the language used to create a Fee Simple Determinable and a Fee Simple Subject to Condition Subsequent.

MAHRENHOLZ v. COUNTY BOARD OF SCHOOL TRUSTEES OF LAWRENCE COUNTY, 417 N.E.2d 138 (Ill. App. 5th Dist., 1981).

JONES, Justice:

This case involves an action to quiet title to real property located in Lawrence County, Illinois. Its resolution depends on the judicial construction of language in a conveyance of that property. The case is before us on the pleadings, plaintiffs' third amended complaint having been dismissed by a final order. The pertinent facts are taken from the pleadings.

On March 18, 1941, W. E. and Jennie Hutton executed a warranty deed in which they conveyed certain land, to be known here as the Hutton School grounds, to the Trustees of School District No. 1, the predecessors of the defendants in this action. The deed provided that "this land to be used for school purpose only; otherwise to revert to Grantors herein." W. E. Hutton died intestate on July 18, 1951, and Jennie Hutton died intestate on February 18, 1969. The Huttons left as their only legal heir their son Harry E. Hutton.

The property conveyed by the Huttons became the site of the Hutton School. Community Unit School District No. 20 succeeded to the grantee of the deed and held classes in the building constructed upon the land until May 30, 1973. After that date, children were transported to classes held at other facilities operated by the District. The District has used the property since then for storage purposes only.

Earl and Madeline Jacqmain executed a warranty deed on October 9, 1959, conveying to the plaintiffs over 390 acres of land in Lawrence County and which included the 40 acre tract from which the Hutton School grounds were taken. When and from whom the Jacqmains acquired the land is not shown and is of no consequence in this appeal. The deed from the Jacqmains to the plaintiffs excepted the Hutton School grounds, but purported to convey the disputed future interest, with the following language:

"Also, except the following tract of land which was on the 18th day of March, 1951, by the said grantors (sic) conveyed to the Trustees of Schools of District No. One (1) of the Town of Allison, in the County of Lawrence and State of Illinois, and described as follows:

(legal description)

and containing one and one-half (1 1/2) acres, more or less; Reversionary interest to Grantees; * * *."

On May 7, 1977, Harry E. Hutton, son and sole heir of W. E. and Jennie Hutton, conveyed to the plaintiffs all of his interest in the Hutton School land. This document was filed in the recorder's office of Lawrence County on September 7, 1977. On September 6, 1977, Harry Hutton disclaimed his interest in the property in favor of the defendants. The disclaimer was in the form of a written document entitled "Disclaimer and Release." It contained the legal description of the Hutton School grounds and recited that Harry E. Hutton disclaimed and released any possibility of reverter or right of entry for condition broken, or other similar interest, in favor of the County Board of School Trustees for Lawrence County, Illinois, successor to the Trustees of School District No. 1 of Lawrence County, Illinois. The document further recited that it was made for the purpose of releasing and extinguishing any right Harry E. Hutton may have had in the "interest retained by W. E. Hutton and Jennie Hutton * * * in that deed to the Trustees of School District No. 1, Lawrence County, Illinois dated March 18, 1941, and filed on the same date * * *." The disclaimer was filed in the recorder's office of Lawrence County on October 4, 1977.

The plaintiffs filed a complaint in the circuit court of Lawrence County on April 9, 1974, in which they sought to quiet title to the school property in themselves, by virtue of the interests acquired from the Jacqmains. This complaint was amended but later dismissed on defendants' motion.

A second amended complaint was filed on September 7, 1977. This alleged that the plaintiffs owned the property through the conveyance from Harry Hutton. The defendants moved to dismiss this complaint because (1) the plaintiffs did not meet the equitable requirements which would entitle them to have title quieted in them and (2) Harry Hutton had no interest in the school property as he never acted to re-enter it. The second amended complaint was dismissed on August 17, 1978, by an order which did not specify the reasons for the decision.

The plaintiffs filed a third amended complaint on September 13, 1978. This complaint recited the interests acquired from the Jacqmains and from Harry Hutton. On March 21, 1979, the trial court entered an order dismissing this complaint. In the order the court found that the

> "(W)arranty deed dated March 18, 1941, from W. E. Hutton and Jennie Hutton to the Trustees of School District No. 1, conveying land here concerned, created a fee simple subject to a condition subsequent followed by the right of entry for condition broken, rather than a determinable fee followed by a possibility of reverter."

Plaintiffs have perfected an appeal to this court.

The basic issue presented by this appeal is whether the trial court correctly concluded that the plaintiffs could not have acquired any interest in the school property from the Jacqmains or from Harry Hutton. Resolution of this issue must turn upon the legal interpretation of the language contained in the March 18, 1941, deed from W. E. and Jennie Hutton to the Trustees of School District No. 1:

> "this land to be used for school purpose only; otherwise to revert to Grantors herein."

In addition to the legal effect of this language we must consider the alienability of the interest created and the effect of subsequent deeds.

The parties appear to be in agreement that the 1941 deed from the Huttons conveyed a defeasible fee simple estate to the grantee, and gave rise to a future interest in the grantors ... and that it did not convey a fee simple absolute, subject to a covenant. The fact that provision was made for forfeiture of the estate conveyed should the land cease to be used for school purposes suggests that this view is correct. [citations omitted]

The future interest remaining in this grantor or his estate can only be a possibility of reverter or a right of re-entry for condition broken. As neither interest may be transferred by will or by inter vivos conveyance (Ill.Rev.Stat., ch. 30, par. 37b), and as the land was being used for school purposes in 1959 when the Jacqmains transferred their interest in the school property to the plaintiffs, the trial court correctly ruled that the plaintiffs could not have acquired any interest in that property from the Jacqmains by the deed of October 9, 1959.

Consequently this court must determine whether the plaintiffs could have acquired an interest in the Hutton School grounds from Harry Hutton. The resolution of this issue depends on the construction of the language of the 1941 deed of the Huttons to the school district. As urged by the defendants and as the trial court found, that deed conveyed a fee simple subject to a condition subsequent followed by a right of re-entry for condition broken. As argued by the plaintiffs, on the other hand, the deed conveyed a fee simple determinable followed by a possibility of reverter. In either case, the grantor and his heirs retain an interest in the property which may become possessory if the condition is broken. We emphasize here that although [Illinois statutory law] provides that rights of re-entry for condition broken and possibilities of reverter are neither alienable or devisable, they are inheritable. … The type of interest held governs the mode of reinvestment with title if reinvestment is to occur. If the grantor had a possibility of reverter, he or his heirs become the owner of the property by operation of law as soon as the condition is broken. If he has a right of re-entry for condition broken, he or his heirs become the owner of the property only after they act to re-take the property.

It is alleged, and we must accept, that classes were last held in the Hutton School in 1973. Harry Hutton, sole heir of the grantors, did not act to legally retake the premises but instead conveyed his interest in that land to the plaintiffs in 1977. If Harry Hutton had only a naked right of re-entry for condition broken, then he could not be the owner of that property until he had legally re-entered the land. Since he took no steps for a legal re-entry, he had only a right of re-entry in 1977, and that right cannot be conveyed inter vivos. On the other hand, if Harry Hutton had a possibility of reverter in the property, then he owned the school property as soon as it ceased to be used for school purposes. Therefore, assuming (1) that cessation of classes constitutes "abandonment of school purposes" on the land, (2) that the conveyance from Harry Hutton to the plaintiffs was legally correct, and (3) that the conveyance was not pre-empted by Hutton's disclaimer in favor of the school district, the plaintiffs could have acquired an interest in the Hutton School grounds if Harry Hutton had inherited a possibility of reverter from his parents.

The difference between a fee simple determinable (or, determinable fee) and a fee simple subject to a condition subsequent, is solely a matter of judicial interpretation of the words of a grant. [citations omitted] As Blackstone explained, there is a fundamental theoretical difference between a conditional estate, such as a fee simple subject to a condition subsequent, and a limited estate, such as a fee simple determinable.

> "A distinction is however made between a condition in deed and a limitation, which Littleton denominates also a condition in law. For when an estate is so expressly confined and limited by the words of it's (sic) creation, that it cannot endure for any longer time than till the contingency happens upon which the estate is to fail, this is denominated in limitation : as when land is granted to a man, so long as he is parson of Dale, or while he continues unmarried, or until out of the rents and profits he shall have made 500 . and the like. In such case the estate determines as soon as the contingency happens (when he ceases to be parson, marries a wife, or has received the 500 .) and the next subsequent estate, which depends upon such determination, becomes immediately vested, without any act to be done by him who is next in expectancy. But when an estate is, strictly speaking, upon condition in deed (as if granted expressly upon condition to be void upon the payment of 40 . by the grantor, or so that the grantee continues unmarried, or provided he goes to York, etc.), the law permits it to endure beyond the time when such contingency happens, unless the grantor or his heir or assigns take advantage of the breach of the condition, and make either an entry or a claim in order to avoid the estate." (Emphasis in original.) 2 W. Blackstone, Commentaries.

A fee simple determinable may be thought of as a limited grant, while a fee simple subject to a condition subsequent is an absolute grant to which a condition is appended. In other words, a grantor should give a fee simple determinable if he intends to give property for so long as it is needed for the purposes for which it is given and no longer, but he should employ a fee simple subject to a condition subsequent if he intends to compel compliance with a condition by penalty of a forfeiture. [citation omitted]

Following Blackstone's examples, the Huttons would have created a fee simple determinable if they had allowed the school district to retain the property so long as or while it was used for school purposes, or until it ceased to be so used. Similarly, a fee simple subject to a condition subsequent would have arisen had the Huttons given the land upon condition that or provided that it be used for school purposes. In the 1941 deed, though the Huttons gave the land "to be used for school purpose only, otherwise to revert to Grantors herein," no words of temporal limitation, or terms of express condition, were used in the grant.

The plaintiffs argue that the word "only" should be construed as a limitation rather than a condition. The defendants respond that where ambiguous language is used in a deed, the courts of Illinois have expressed a constructional preference for a fee simple subject to a condition subsequent. [citation omitted] Both sides refer us to cases involving deeds which contain language analogous to the 1941 grant in this case.

We believe that a close analysis of the wording of the original grant shows that the grantors intended to create a fee simple determinable followed by a possibility of reverter. Here, the use of the word "only" immediately following the grant "for school purpose" demonstrates that the Huttons wanted to give the land to the school district only as long as it was needed and no longer. The language "this land to be used for school purpose only" is an example of a grant which contains a limitation within the granting clause. It suggests a limited grant, rather than a full grant subject to a condition, and thus, both theoretically and linguistically, gives rise to a fee simple determinable.

The second relevant clause furnishes plaintiffs' position with additional support. It cannot be argued that the phrase "otherwise to revert to grantors herein" is inconsistent with a fee simple subject to a condition subsequent. Nor does the word "revert" automatically create a possibility of reverter. But, in combination with the preceding phrase, the provisions by which possession is returned to the grantors seem to trigger a mandatory return rather than a permissive return because it is not stated that the grantor "may" re-enter the land. [citation omitted]

The terms used in the 1941 deed, although imprecise, were designed to allow the property to be used for a single purpose, namely, for "school purpose." The Huttons intended to have the land back if it were ever used otherwise. Upon a grant of exclusive use followed by an express provision for reverter when that use ceases, courts and commentators have agreed that a fee simple determinable, rather than a fee simple subject to a condition subsequent, is created. [citation omitted] Our own research has uncovered cases from other jurisdictions and sources in which language very similar to that in the Hutton deed has been held to create a fee simple determinable:

> "A conveyance 'for the use, intent and purpose of a site for a School House * * * (and) whenever the said School District removes the School House from said tract of land or whenever said School House ceases to be used as the Public School House * * * then the said Trust shall cease and determine and the said land shall revert to the grantor and his heirs.'" Consolidated School District v. Walter (1954), 243 Minn. 159, 66 N.W.2d 881, 882.

> "(I)t being absolutely understood that when said land ceases to be used for school purposes it is to revert to the above grantor, his heirs." U.S. v. 1119.15 Acres of Land, (E.D.Ill.1942), 44 F.Supp. 449.

> "That I, S.S. Gray (Widower), for and in consideration of the sum of Donation to Wheeler School District to be used by said Wheeler Special School District for school and church purposes and to revert to me should school and church be discontinued or moved." Williams v. Kirby School District (Ark. 1944), 181 S.W.2d 488, 490.

> "It is understood and agreed that if the above described land is abandoned by the said

second parties and not used for school purposes then the above described land reverts to the party of the first part." School District No. 6 v. Russell (1964), 156 Colo. 75, 396 P.2d 929, 930.

"(T)o B and C (trustees of a school district) and their heirs and successors for school purposes and to revert to the grantor when it ceases to be so used." Restatement of Property, sec. 44, comment 1, illustration V (1936).

Thus, authority from this state and others indicates that the grant in the Hutton deed did in fact create a fee simple determinable. We are not persuaded by the cases cited by the defendants for the terms of conveyance in those cases distinguish them from the facts presented here.

In Board of Education of Normal School District v. Trustees of the First Baptist Church of Normal (1872), 63 Ill. 204, the deed provided that the property was to be used for church purposes only, but when it ceased to be so used, the trustees were to pay the grantor $200, and the grantees would then have an absolute title. This is certainly no authority for this case because no interest in the land beyond the receipt of $200 was created in the grantor.

The deed in Sherman v. Town of Jefferson (1916), 274 Ill. 294, 113 N.E. 624, stated,

"This conveyance is made, understood and agreed by and between the parties hereto upon the express condition the premises conveyed shall be occupied, used and enjoyed for town purposes only, and upon ceasing to be so used and enjoyed by the said party of the second part, in whole or in any part thereof, the conveyance above becomes and remains absolutely void and of no longer force, effect or obligation as against the said party of the first part, his heirs and assigns." 274 Ill. 294, 295, 113 N.E. 624, 625.

This conveyance may be distinguished from the Hutton deed because the reversion clause in Sherman provided that the grant would, upon breach of condition, be void only against the grantor. This unusual language is merely another way to state that the grantee may retain possession until the grantor re-enters the property.

The estate created in Latham v. Illinois Central Railroad Co. (1912), 253 Ill. 93, 97 N.E. 254, was held to be a fee simple subject to a condition subsequent. Land was conveyed to a railroad in return for the railroad's agreement to erect and maintain a passenger depot and a freight depot on the premises. The deed was made to the grantee, "their successors and assigns forever, for the uses and purposes hereinafter mentioned and for NONE other." Those purposes were limited to "railroad purposes only." The deed provided "that in case of non-user of said premises so conveyed for the uses and purposes aforesaid, that then and in that case the title to said premises shall revert back to (the grantors), their heirs, executors, administrators and assigns." The property was granted to the railroad to have and hold forever, "subject, nevertheless, to all the conditions, covenants, agreements and limitations in this deed expressed." The estate in Latham may be distinguished from that created here in that the former was a grant "forever" which was subjected to certain use restrictions while the Hutton deed gave the property to the school district only as long as it could use it.

In Northwestern University v. Wesley Memorial Hospital (1919), 290 Ill. 205, 125 N.E. 13, a conveyance was "made upon the express condition that said Wesley Hospital, the grantee herein, shall erect a hospital building on said lot * * * and that on the failure of said Wesley Hospital to carry out these conditions the title shall revert to Northwestern University." This language cannot be interpreted as creating anything but a fee simple subject to a condition subsequent, and the court so held.

The defendants also direct our attention to the case of McElvain v. Dorris (1921), 298 Ill. 377, 131 N.E. 608. There, land was sold subject to the following condition: "This tract of land is to be used for mill purposes, and if not used for mill purposes the title reverts back to the former owner." When the mill was abandoned, the heirs of the grantor brought suit in ejectment and were successful. The Supreme Court of Illinois did not mention the possibility that the quoted words could have created a fee simple determinable but instead stated,

> "Annexed to the grant there was a condition subsequent, by a breach of which there would be a right of re-entry by the grantor or her heirs at law. (Citations.) A breach of the condition in such a case does not, of itself, determine the estate, but an entry, or some act equivalent thereto, is necessary to revest the estate, and bringing a suit in ejectment is equivalent to such re-entry." 298 Ill. at 379, 131 N.E. 608.

It is urged by the defendants that McElvain v. Dorris stands for the proposition that the quoted language in the deed creates a fee simple subject to a condition subsequent. We must agree with the defendants that the grant in McElvain is strikingly similar to that in this case. However, the opinion in McElvain is ambiguous in several respects. First, that portion of the opinion which states that "Annexed to the grant there was a condition subsequent * * *" may refer to the provision quoted above, or it may refer to another provision not reproduced in that opinion. Second, even if the court's reference is to the quoted language, the holding may reflect only the court's acceptance of the parties' construction of the grant. (A similar procedure was followed in Trustees of Schools v. Batdorf (1955), 6 Ill.2d 486, 130 N.E.2d 111, as noted by defendants.) After all, as an action in ejectment was brought in McElvain, the difference between a fee simple determinable and a fee simple subject to a condition subsequent would have no practical effect and the court did not discuss it.

To the extent that McElvain holds that the quoted language establishes a fee simple subject to a condition subsequent, it is contrary to the weight of Illinois and American authority. A more appropriate case with which to resolve the problem presented here is North v. Graham (1908), 235 Ill. 178, 85 N.E. 267. Land was conveyed to trustees of a church under a deed which stated that "said tract of land above described to revert to the party of the first part whenever it ceases to be used or occupied for a meeting house or church." Following an extended discussion of determinable fees, the court concluded that such an estate is legal in Illinois and that the language of the deed did in fact create that estate.

North v. Graham, like this case, falls somewhere between those cases in which appears the classic language used to create a fee simple determinable and that used to create a fee simple subject to a condition subsequent. The language used classically to create a fee simple determinable is "so long as it is used for * * *," as may be seen in [citations omitted].

The language used typically to create a fee simple subject to a condition subsequent is, variously, "provided it be used for * * *," O'Donnell v. Robson (1909), 239 Ill. 634, 88 N.E. 175; "that in case of breach of these covenants * * * said premises shall immediately revert * * *," Storke v. Penn Mutual Life Ins. Co. (1945), 390 Ill. 619, 61 N.E.2d 552; "and, if this agreement is broken, said land shall revert * * *," Wakefield v. Van Tassell (1903), 202 Ill. 41, 66 N.E. 830, writ of error dismissed, 192 U.S. 601, 24 S.Ct. 850, 48 L.Ed. 583; "in the event the (grantee) shall fail to perform * * * all the above requirements and conditions, all the lands * * * shall revert * * *," Gray v. Chicago, Milw. and St. Paul Rwy. Co. (1901), 189 Ill. 400, 59 N.E. 950.

Although the word "whenever" is used in the North v. Graham deed, it is not found in a granting clause, but in a reverter clause. The court found this slightly unorthodox construction sufficient to create a fee simple determinable, and we believe that the word "only" placed in the granting clause of the Hutton deed brings this case under the rule of North v. Graham.

We hold, therefore, that the 1941 deed from W. E. and Jennie Hutton to the Trustees of School District No. 1 created a fee simple determinable in the Trustees followed by a possibility of reverter in the Huttons and their heirs. Accordingly, the trial court erred in dismissing plaintiffs' third amended complaint which followed its holding that the plaintiffs could not have acquired any interest in the Hutton School property from Harry Hutton. We must therefore reverse and remand this cause to the trial court for further proceedings.

We refrain from deciding the following issues: (1) whether the 1977 conveyance from Harry Hutton was legally sufficient to pass his interest in the school property to the plaintiffs, (2) whether Harry Hutton effectively disclaimed his interest in the property in favor of the defendants by virtue of his 1977 disclaimer, and (3) whether the defendants have ceased to use the Hutton School grounds for "school purposes." [citations omitted]

REVERSED and REMANDED.

KARNS and HARRISON, JJ., concur.

Why did it matter which type of estate was created by the Hutton deed?

If the Huttons created a Fee Simple Determinable, then ownership of the Hutton School Grounds would have been as follows:

March 1941 (original deed)

Trustees of School District No. 1 has Fee Simple Determinable.

W.E. and Jennie Hutton have Possibility of Reverter.

July 1941

W.E. and Jennie Hutton purport to convey reversionary interest but cannot because Possibilities of Reverter could not be conveyed in Illinois in 1941.

1951

W.E. Hutton dies intestate. Jennie Hutton inherits his share of the Possibility of Reverter.

October 1959

Jacqmain conveyance to Mahrenholz doesn't matter because they didn't own the interest.

1969

Jennie Hutton dies. Harry Hutton is sole heir. Harry inherits the Possibility of Reverter.

May 1973

School District stops holding classes. If we assume that is a breach of the condition, then property automatically goes to Harry Hutton in Fee Simple Absolute.

May 1977

Harry Hutton conveyed Fee Simple Absolute to Mahrenholz.

September 1977

Harry Hutton disclaimed, but he had nothing left.

If the Huttons created a Fee Simple Subject to Condition Subsequent, then ownership of the Hutton School Grounds would have been as follows:

March 1941 (original deed)

Trustees of School District No. 1 has Fee Simple Subject to Condition Subsequent.

W.E. and Jennie Hutton have Right of Entry.

July 1941

W.E. and Jennie Hutton purport to convey reversionary interest but cannot because Rights of Entry could not be conveyed in Illinois in 1941.

1951

W.E. Hutton dies intestate. Jennie Hutton inherits his share of the Right of Entry.

October 1959

Jacqmain conveyance to Mahrenholz doens't matter because they didn't own the interest.

1969

Jennie Hutton dies. Harry Hutton is sole heir. Harry takes the Right of Entry.

May 1973

School District stops holding classes. If we assume this is a breach of the condition, then Harry's Right of Entry is activated.

May 1977

Harry Hutton tried to convey to Mahrenholz but couldn't convey Right of Entry under Illinois law.

September 1977

Harry Hutton disclaimed Right of Entry to the School District.

CHAPTER 10
REMAINDERS

1. Definition

A **Remainder** is a Future Interest in a party other than the original grantor that:

(1) is capable of becoming possessory immediately upon the expiration of the prior estate; and

(2) does not divest (or cut short) any interest in a prior transferee.

The guaranty of possession is not required; the *possibility* of possession is enough.

A Remainder "waits patiently" for the preceding Estate to expire before it becomes possessory. This means that Remainders can only follow the Finite Estates. They cannot follow Defeasible Fees because Defeasible Fees do not naturally expire; they are cut short by the intervention of a condition subsequent.

There are four kinds of Remainders:

- Contingent Remainder
- Indefeasibly Vested Remainder
- Vested Remainder Subject to Divestment
- Vested Remainder Subject to Open

2. Contingent Remainders

A **Contingent Remainder** is one in which the remainderman's right to immediate possession is *subject to a condition precedent* (other than the natural expiration of the prior Finite Estate). Recall that we don't label Reversions as "vested" or "contingent," but the Reversion could be thought of as contingent on the failure of the condition precedent described in the original Contingent Remainder.

There are three ways that a Remainder can be contingent:

(1) It is subject to the **occurrence of some stated event**.

(2) It is conveyed to **unascertained persons** who are described rather than named.

(3) It is conveyed to **unborn persons**.

If the first future interest is a Contingent Remainder, it is necessarily true that another third party will have a Contingent Remainder or the original grantor will have a Reversion. If two Contingent Remainders are created, they are referred to as "**alternative contingent remainders**."

O CONVEYS BLACKACRE TO A FOR LIFE

Example 1

O conveys Blackacre to A for life, remainder to B and her heirs if B marries C.

A has a Life Estate

B has a Contingent Remainder in Fee Simple Absolute.

O has a Reversion in Fee Simple Absolute.

Note: B has a Contingent Remainder because it is subject to an express condition precedent, i.e. the marriage of B and C.

Example 2

O devises Blackacre to A for life, remainder to the reigning King or Queen of the United Kingdom in 2050.

A has a Life Estate

The reigning King or Queen of the UK in 2050 has a Contingent Remainder in Fee Simple Absolute.

O's Estate has a Contingent Remainder in Fee Simple Absolute.

Note: This is a Contingent Remainder because it is in favor of an unascertained person. In 2050, we will need to see if there is a King or Queen and, if so, identify the owner of the Future Interest. It is possible that there will be no King or Queen in 2050 and that the condition precedent will fail. In that case, Blackacre would revert to O. Example 2 creates alternative contingent remainders.

Example 3

O conveys Blackacre to A for life, remainder to B's next born child.

A has a Life Estate

B's next born child has a Contingent Remainder in Fee Simple Absolute.

O has a Reversion in Fee Simple Absolute.

Note: This is a Contingent Remainder because it is possible that B will never have a child after the conveyance and, therefore, the condition precedent will fail.

Example 4

O conveys to A for life, then to B for life.

A has a Life Estate

B has an Indefeasibly Vested Remainder in Fee Simple Absolute.

O has a Reversion in Fee Simple Absolute.

There is an implicit condition precedent attached to B's future interest—B must survive A to take advantage of the Life Estate. General rules would likely label B's future interest as a Contingent Remainder. However, the weight of authority holds that unless that condition precedent is expressly stated, B holds an Indefeasibly Vested Remainder in Fee Simple Absolute.

Example 5

O conveys to A for life, then, if B survives A, to B for life.

> *A has a Life Estate*
>
> *B has a Contingent Remainder in Fee Simple Absolute.*
>
> *O has a Reversion in Fee Simple Absolute.*

The only difference between Example 4 and Example 5 is that the condition precedent attached to B's remainder is expressly stated.

3. Indefeasibly Vested Remainder

An **Indefeasibly Vested Remainder** is one in which the remainderman's right to immediate possession is *without pre-condition* (except the natural expiration of the prior Present Estate). In other words, the Remainder must be *certain* to become a possessory Estate in order to be an Indefeasibly Vested Remainder. Note that unlike a Contingent Remainder, an Indefeasibly Vested Remainder does not have a corresponding Contingent Remainder or Reversion because there is no possibility that it will not become possessory.

Example 6

O conveys Blackacre to A for life, remainder to B and his heirs.

> *A has a Life Estate.*
>
> *B has an Indefeasibly Vested Remainder in Fee Simple Absolute.*

Note: It is irrelevant whether or not B is alive when A dies. If B dies before A, B's Remainder will pass via devise or via descent.

4. Vested Remainder Subject to Divestment

A **Vested Remainder Subject to Divestment** is sometimes also referred to as a Vested Remainder Subject to Defeasance. It is sometimes difficult to tell the difference between a Contingent Remainder, a Vested Remainder Subject to Divestment, or a Defeasible Fee. All three have conditions attached. A Contingent Remainder has a condition precedent to *vesting*. A Vested Remainder Subject to Divestment has no condition precedent to vesting but has a condition precedent to *possession*. A Defeasible Fee has a condition *subsequent* to possession. If the condition precedent fails for either type of Remainder, the Future Interest never becomes possessory—the difference is whether the Remainder vests before the condition precedent is triggered. This difference mattered historically because Contingent Remainders were less valuable than vested Remainders or subject to different rules regarding their ability to be transferred via conveyance, devise, or descent. In addition, Contingent Remainders are vulnerable to the Rule Against Perpetuities, while Vested Remainders Subject to Divestment are not.

If the first future interest is a Vested Remainder Subject to Divestment, the other future interests in grantees will be Executory Interests because they will operate to cut short the vested remainder.

Example 7

O conveys Blackacre to A for life, then to B, but if B fails to survive A, then to C.

A has a Life Estate

B has a Vested Remainder Subject to Divestment in Fee Simple Absolute

C has an Executory Interest in Fee Simple Absolute

Note that the requirement that B survive A is phrased as a *condition subsequent* to vesting. In other words, the conveyance language gives B the Remainder "then to B" and *then* imposes the condition, "but if B fails to survive A." Contrast this with "O conveys Blackacre to A for life, then if B survives A, to B, and if not, to C." In this second example, the conveyance language phrases the identical requirement as a *condition precedent* to vesting. The different between the two is essentially that if the remainder is contingent if the conditional element is incorporated into the description of or into the estate of the remainderman, however, if after giving a vested interest, a clause is added which creates a possibility that it may be divested, the remainder is vested subject to divestment. If the language is ambiguous, the applicable rule of construction will construe in favor of a vested remainder subject to divestment because the law generally favors the vesting of estates.

In both examples, C's Future Interest is subject to an express condition precedent and is therefore a Contingent Remainder. A Vested Remainder Subject to Divestment will always be paired with an Executory Interest in a third party or a Reversion in favor of the original grantor.

Example 8

O devises Blackacre to A for life, remainder to B but if B dies during A's lifetime, then to C.

A has a Life Estate

B has a Vested Remainder Subject to Divestment in Fee Simple Absolute

C has an Executory Interest in Fee Simple Absolute

5. Vested Remainder Subject to Open

A Vested Remainder Subject to Open is sometimes referred to as a Vested Remainder Subject to Partial Divestment. A Remainder is Vested Subject to Open if it is subject to no conditions precedent and when it is in favor of a class that contains at least one member and is still capable of adding future members (i.e. it is "open"). It is only the existing class members that have a Vested Remainder Subject to Open. Unborn or unascertained potential class members have Contingent Remainders.

Example 6

O conveys Blackacre to A for life, remainder to B's children. At the time of the conveyance, B is alive and has two children, X and Y.

A has a Life Estate

X and Y have Vested Remainders Subject to Open in Fee Simple Absolute

Potential children of B have Contingent Remainders in Fee Simple Absolute [Some authorities refer to the interest held by the potential children of B as Shifting Executory Interests because once they are born, they will partially divest X and Y.]

Note that the class (i.e. "B's children") closes when B dies.

Example 7

O conveys Blackacre to A for life, remainder to B's children alive at B's death. At the time of the conveyance, B is alive and has two children, X and Y.

A has a Life Estate.

X, Y, and Potential children of B have a Contingent Remainder in Fee Simple Absolute.

O has a Reversion.

Note the difference between Example 6 and Example 7 is that in Example 6, the class—B's children—has two confirmed members—X and Y. They have been born and need to do nothing else for their remainders to become possessory. They only question is how large their share of Blackacre will be. They would currently share Blackacre 50/50. But if another child is born to B, their share of Blackacre will be reduced.

In Example 7, there are no confirmed members of the class—B's children alive at B's death—because B is still alive. It is not certain that X or Y will receive anything—they could die before B. Because it is possible that B could die with no living children, it is possible for Blackacre to return to O. Therefore there is a Reversion to O in Example 7, but there is no Reversion in Example 6.

CHAPTER 11
PROBLEM SET INSTRUCTIONS

There are four problem sets in this book. The first three are designed to allow you to methodically work through the Finite Estates (Problem Set I), the Defeasible Fees (Problem Set II), and the types of Remainder (Problem Set III).

The first two problem sets are designed to be completed in two stages. I suggest that you become comfortable with the Present Estates before delving into the different kinds of Remainders and Executory Interests. So, for example, with Problem Set I, identify who holds each Present Estate and the type of Present Estate after reviewing the rules of the Finite Estates. Then, after learning about the different types of Remainders, go back to Problem Set I and complete all steps in the Analytical Framework below.

Problem Sets I-III identify each of the parties in the problem and prompt you to identify the relevant Present Estate or Future Interest, as applicable. Problem Set IV contains no prompts and is designed to be completed as a review to confirm that you understand all of the rules.

Analytical Framework

To solve Present Estates and Future Interests problems, I suggest that you methodically apply the following analytical framework, solving each step in order:

1. Identify who holds the Present Estate.
2. Identify which Present Estate has been created.
3. Identify who holds the first Future Interest.
4. Identify which Future Interest has been created.
5. Indicate the duration of the Future Interest (i.e. what kind of Present Estate will the Future Interest become if and when it becomes possessory?)
6. Identify if there is a second Future Interest and, if so, who holds it.
7. Identify which Future Interest has been created.
8. Indicate the duration of the Future Interest.
9. Repeat the analysis of Future Interests as necessary.

CHAPTER 12

PROBLEM SET I: FINITE ESTATES

Instructions:

1. After reviewing the material on Finite Estates, solve these problems identifying ONLY the present estate held by A. Answers for the Present Estates can be found in Chapter 16.

2. After reviewing the materials on Future Interests, solve these problems identifying the future interest retained by O or granted to a third party. Answers for both the Present Estates and the Future Interests can be found in Chapter 17.

1. **O conveys Blackacre to A for life.**

   A has: _____

   O has: _____

2. **O devises Blackacre to A for life.**

   A has: _____

   O's Estate has: _____

3. **O conveys Blackacre to A for life, then to B and her heirs.**

   A has: _____

   B has: _____

   O has: _____

4. O conveys Blackacre to A for life, then to B for life.

A has: _____

B has: _____

O has: _____

5. O devises Blackacre to A for life, then to B for life.

A has: _____

B has: _____

O's Estate has: _____

6. O conveys Blackacre to A for life, then to B for life, then to C.

A has: _____

B has: _____

C has: _____

O has: _____

7. O conveys Blackacre to A and the heirs of her body.

A has: _____

O has: _____

8. O devises Blackacre to A and the heirs of her body.

A has: _____

O's Estate has: _____

9. O conveys Blackacre to A and the heirs of her body, then to B and her heirs.

A has: _____

B has: _____

O has: _____

10. O conveys Blackacre to A for ten years.

A has: _____

O has: _____

11. O conveys Blackacre to A for ten years, then to B and her heirs.

A has: _____

B has: _____

O has: _____

12. O conveys Blackacre to A for ten years, then to B for life, then to C and his heirs.

A has: _____

B has: _____

C has: _____

O has: _____

13. O conveys Blackacre to A for life, then to A's children. A has one child, X.

A has: _____

X has: _____

A's children have: _____

O has: _____

14. O conveys Blackacre to A for life, then to B and her heirs. A then conveys her estate to C.

A has: _____

B has: _____

C has: _____

15. O conveys Blackacre to A for ten years, then to the person who is then host of The Tonight Show.

A has: _____

The host has: _____

O has: _____

16. O conveys Blackacre to A for ten years, then to B and his heirs if B gets married before A's estate ends.

A has: _____

B has: _____

O has: _____

17. O conveys Blackacre to A for life, then to B and her heirs, but if B does not survive A, then to C.

A has: _____

B has: _____

C has: _____

O has: _____

18. O conveys Blackacre "to A for life, remainder to B if B survives A, but if not, to C and her heirs."

A has: _____

B has: _____

C has: _____

O has: _____

19. O conveys Blackacre to A for life, then to B and her heirs for so long as B remains unmarried, then to C and her heirs.

A has: _____

B has: _____

C has: _____

O has: _____

20. O conveys Blackacre to A for life, then to B and her heirs if B graduates from law school before A dies, but if B fails to graduate from law school before A dies, then to C and his heirs.

A has: _____

B has: _____

C has: _____

O has: _____

O CONVEYS BLACKACRE TO A FOR LIFE

CHAPTER 13

PROBLEM SET II: DEFEASIBLE FEES

Instructions:

1. After reviewing the material on the Defeasible Fees, solve these problems identifying ONLY the Present Estate held by A. Answers for the Present Estates can be found in Chapter 18.

2. After reviewing the materials on Future Interests, solve these problems identifying the future interest retained by O or granted to a third party. Answers for both the Present Estates and the Future Interests can be found in Chapter 19.

1. O conveys Blackacre to A and her heirs so long as Blackacre is used for educational purposes.

   A has: _____

   O has: _____

2. O conveys Blackacre to A and her heirs, but if Blackacre is no longer used for educational purposes, then O has the right to reclaim Blackacre.

   A has: _____

   O has: _____

3. O conveys Blackacre to A and her heirs so long as Blackacre continues to be used for agricultural purposes, then to B and her heirs.

   A has: _____

   B has: _____

   O has: _____

4. **O conveys Blackacre to A and her heirs, but if Blackacre is used for commercial purposes, then to B and her heirs.**

A has: _____

B has: _____

O has: _____

5. **O conveys Blackacre to A and her heirs, unless Blackacre is used for commercial purposes.**

A has: _____

O has: _____

6. **O conveys Blackacre to A provided that he graduates from college before taking possession.**

A has: _____

O has: _____

7. **O conveys Blackacre to A for life, then to B and her heirs so long as Blackacre continues to be farmed organically.**

A has: _____

B has: _____

O has: _____

8. **O conveys Blackacre to A for life, then to B and her heirs, but if Blackacre is used for commercial purposes following A's life estate, then to C and her heirs.**

A has: _____

B has: _____

C has: _____

O has: _____

9. O conveys Blackacre to A and her heirs until B graduates from college, then to B and her heirs.

A has: _____
B has: _____
O has: _____

10. O devises to A and her heirs while the property is used for charitable purposes.

A has: _____
O has: _____
O's Estate has. _____

11. O conveys Blackacre to A and his heirs, but if A allows liquor to be sold on Blackacre, to B if B is then living, and if B is not then living, to C and his heirs.

A has: _____
B has: _____
C has: _____
O has: _____

12. O conveys Blackacre "to A and her heirs, on the express condition that Blackacre be used only for residential purposes."

A has: _____
O has: _____

13. O conveys Blackacre "to A and her heirs, it being my wish that Blackacre be used only for residential purposes."

A has: _____

O has: _____

14. O conveys Blackacre "to A, provided that the estate hereby granted to A shall automatically terminate if liquor is sold, used, or stored on the premises."

A has: _____

O's Estate has: _____

15. O devises Blackacre "to A, for so long as A continues to live on Blackacre."

A has: _____

O's Estate has: _____

CHAPTER 14

PROBLEM SET III: REMAINDERS

Instructions:

Problem Set III focuses on the types of Remainders. Answers for both the Present Estates and the Future Interests can be found in Chapter 20.

1. O conveys Blackacre to A for life, then if B is still living, to B and her heirs, but if B predeceases A, then to C and her heirs.

A has:_____

B has:_____

C has:_____

O has:_____

2. O conveys Blackacre to A for life, then to B and his heirs if B goes straight from high school to college before A's death, and if B fails to do so, to C and her heirs.

A has:_____

B has:_____

C has:_____

3. O conveys Blackacre to A for life, then to A's children and their heirs. At the time of the conveyance, A has one child, X.

A has:_____

X has:_____

A's unborn children have:_____

O has:_____

4. O conveys Blackacre to A for life, then to B.

A has: _____

B has: _____

O has: _____

5. O conveys Blackacre to A for life, then to B and his heirs if B lives to the age of 30. (Assume that B is currently age 25.)

A has: _____

B has: _____

O has: _____

6. O conveys Blackacre to A for life, then to B's children and their heirs. B has no children at the time of the conveyance.

A has: _____

B has: _____

B's children have: _____

O has: _____

7. O devises Blackacre to A for life, then, if B survives A, to B, but if B does not survive A, then to C.

A has: _____

B has: _____

C has: _____

O has: _____

8. O conveys Blackacre to A for life, then to B for life, then to C's children. Assume that C is alive at the time of the conveyance and has one child, M.

A has: _____

B has: _____

C has: _____

M has: _____

C's unborn children have: _____

O has: _____

9. O conveys Blackacre to A for ten years, then to the then-current Governor of North Carolina.

A has: _____

The then-current Governor of NC has: _____

O has: _____

10. O devises Blackacre to A for life, then to B and his heirs if B gets married before A dies.

A has: _____

B has: _____

O's Estate has: _____

11. O conveys Blackacre to A for life, then to B and her heirs as long as Blackacre continues to be farmed organically.

A has: _____

B has: _____

O has: _____

12. O devises Blackacre to A for life, then to B and his heirs if B survives A.

A has: _____
B has: _____
O's Estate has: _____

13. O conveys Blackacre to A for life, then to B for life, then to C and her heirs if C quits smoking before B dies.

A has: _____
B has: _____
C has: _____
O has: _____

14. O devises Blackacre to A for two years, then to B for life, then to C and her heirs as long as Blackacre is used for charitable purposes, any remaining interest to D and his heirs.

A has: _____
B has: _____
C has: _____
D has: _____
O's Estate has: _____

15. O conveys Blackacre "to A for life, then to return to me for life, then to C."

A has: _____
C has: _____
O has: _____

16. O conveys Blackacre to A for ten years, then to B for life, then to B's heirs.

A has:_____

B has:_____

B's heirs have:_____

O has:_____

CHAPTER 15

PROBLEM SET IV: REVIEW

Instructions:

Answers for both the Present Estates and the Future Interests can be found in Chapter 21.

1. O conveys Blackacre to A.

2. O devises Blackacre to A.

3. O conveys Blackacre to A for life.

4. O devises Blackacre to A for life.

5. O conveys Blackacre to A for life, then to B.

6. O conveys Blackacre to A and the heirs of her body.

7. O devises Blackacre to A and the heirs of her body.

8. O conveys Blackacre to A and the heirs of her body, then to B.

9. O conveys Blackacre to A for a period of two years.

10. O devises Blackacre to A for a period of two years.

11. O conveys Blackacre to A for a period of two years, then to B.

12. O conveys Blackacre to A as long as Blackacre is used as a cat sanctuary.

13. O devises Blackacre to A as long as Blackacre is used as a cat sanctuary.

14. O conveys Blackacre to A as long as Blackacre it used as a cat sanctuary, then to B.

15. O conveys Blackacre to A, provided that dogs are not allowed on Blackacre.

16. O devises Blackacre to A, provided that dogs are not allowed on Blackacre.

17. O conveys Blackacre to A, provided that dogs are not allowed on Blackacre, thereafter to B.

18. O conveys Blackacre to A, provided that dogs are not allowed on Blackacre, and if dogs are allowed on Blackacre, B shall have the right to enter and take possession.

19. O conveys Blackacre to A if and when A graduates from law school.

20. O devises Blackacre to A if and when A graduates from law school.

21. O conveys Blackacre to A but if B graduates from law school, to B.

22. O conveys Blackacre to A for life, then to B only if B promises to never, ever allow dogs on Blackacre.

23. O devises Blackacre to A for life, then to B only if B promises to never, ever allow dogs on Blackacre.

24. O conveys Blackacre to A for life, then to B only if B promises to never, ever allow dogs on Blackacre and then only so long as no dogs are allowed on Blackacre.

25. O conveys Blackacre to A for life, then to B only if B promises to never, ever allow dogs on Blackacre and then only so long as no dogs are allowed on Blackacre, and if B fails to promise or if dogs are ever allowed on Blackacre, then to C.

26. O conveys Blackacre to A for life, then to A's oldest living child at the time of A's death. A has three children at the time of the conveyance: X, Y, and Z.

27. O devises Blackacre to A for life, then to A's oldest living child at the time of A's death. A has three children at the time of the conveyance: X, Y, and Z.

28. O conveys Blackacre to A for life, then to A's then-living children. A has three children at the time of the conveyance: X, Y, and Z.

29. O devises Blackacre to A for life, then to A's then-living children. A has three children at the time of the conveyance: X, Y, and Z.

30. O conveys Blackacre to A for life, then to A's children. A has three children at the time of the conveyance: X, Y, and Z.

31. O devises Blackacre to A for life, then to A's children. A has three children at the time of the devise: X, Y, and Z.

32. O conveys Blackacre to A for life, then to A's children for life, then to A's grandchildren. At the time of the conveyance, A has one child, X, and no grandchildren.

33. O conveys Blackacre to A for life, then to A's children for life, then to A's grandchildren. At the time of the conveyance, A has one child, X, and one grandchild, M.

CHAPTER 16

PROBLEM SET I: FINITE ESTATES

ANSWERS FOR PRESENT ESTATES ONLY

1. O conveys Blackacre to A for life.

A has a Life Estate

2. O devises Blackacre to A for life.

A has a Life Estate

3. O conveys Blackacre to A for life, then to B and her heirs.

A has a Life Estate

4. O conveys Blackacre to A for life, then to B for life.

A has a Life Estate

5. O devises Blackacre to A for life, then to B for life.

A has a Life Estate

6. O conveys Blackacre to A for life, then to B for life, then to C.

A has a Life Estate

7. O conveys Blackacre to A and the heirs of her body.

A has a Fee Tail

8. O devises Blackacre to A and the heirs of her body.

A has a Fee Tail

9. O conveys Blackacre to A and the heirs of her body, then to B and her heirs.

A has a Fee Tail

10. O conveys Blackacre to A for ten years.

A has a Term of Years

11. O conveys Blackacre to A for ten years, then to B and her heirs.

A has a Term of Years

12. O conveys Blackacre to A for ten years, then to B for life, then to C and his heirs.

A has a Term of Years

13. O conveys Blackacre to A for life, then to A's children. A has one child, X.

A has a Life Estate

14. O conveys Blackacre to A for life, then to B and her heirs. A then conveys her estate to C.

A has a Life Estate

15. O conveys Blackacre to A for ten years, then to the person who is then host of The Tonight Show.

A has a Term of Years

16. O conveys Blackacre to A for ten years, then to B and his heirs if B gets married before A's estate ends.

A has a Term of Years

17. O conveys Blackacre to A for life, then to B and her heirs, but if B does not survive A, then to C.

A has a Life Estate

18. O conveys Blackacre "to A for life, remainder to B if B survives A, but if not, to C and her heirs."

A has a Life Estate

19. O conveys Blackacre to A for life, then to B and her heirs for so long as B remains unmarried, then to C and her heirs.

A has a Life Estate

20. O conveys Blackacre to A for life, then to B and her heirs if B graduates from law school before A dies, but if B fails to graduate from law school before A dies, then to C and his heirs.

A has a Life Estate

CHAPTER 17
PROBLEM SET I: FINITE ESTATES
COMPLETE ANSWERS

1. **O conveys Blackacre to A for life.**

A has a Life Estate

O has a Reversion in Fee Simple Absolute

2. **O devises Blackacre to A for life.**

A has a Life Estate

O's Estate has an Indefeasibly Vested Remainder in Fee Simple Absolute

3. **O conveys Blackacre to A for life, then to B and her heirs.**

A has a Life Estate

B has an Indefeasibly Vested Remainder in Fee Simple Absolute

4. **O conveys Blackacre to A for life, then to B for life.**

A has a Life Estate

B has an Indefeasibly Vested Remainder in Life Estate

O has a Reversion in Fee Simple Absolute

5. **O devises Blackacre to A for life, then to B for life.**

A has a Life Estate

B has an Indefeasibly Vested Remainder in Life Estate

O's Estate has an Indefeasibly Vested Remainder in Fee Simple Absolute

6. **O conveys Blackacre to A for life, then to B for life, then to C.**

A has a Life Estate

B has an Indefeasibly Vested Remainder in Life Estate

C has an Indefeasibly Vested Remainder in Fee Simple Absolute

7. **O conveys Blackacre to A and the heirs of her body.**

A has a Fee Tail

O has a Reversion in Fee Simple Absolute

8. **O devises Blackacre to A and the heirs of her body.**

A has a Fee Tail

O's Estate has an Indefeasibly Vested Remainder in Fee Simple Absolute

9. **O conveys Blackacre to A and the heirs of her body, then to B and her heirs.**

A has a Fee Tail

B has an Indefeasibly Vested Remainder in Fee Simple Absolute

10. **O conveys Blackacre to A for ten years.**

A has a Term of Years

O has a Reversion in Fee Simple Absolute

11. **O conveys Blackacre to A for ten years, then to B and her heirs.**

A has a Term of Years

B has an Indefeasibly Vested Remainder in Fee Simple Absolute

12. **O conveys Blackacre to A for ten years, then to B for life, then to C and his heirs.**

A has a Term of Years

B has an Indefeasibly Vested Remainder in Life Estate

C has an Indefeasibly Vested Remainder in Fee Simple Absolute

13. **O conveys Blackacre to A for life, then to A's children. A has one child, X.**

A has a Life Estate

X has a Vested Remainder Subject to Open in Fee Simple Absolute

A's children have Contingent Remainders in Fee Simple Absolute

14. **O conveys Blackacre to A for life, then to B and her heirs. A then conveys her estate to C.**

A has a Life Estate

B has an Indefeasibly Vested Remainder in Fee Simple Absolute

After the conveyance from A to C:

C has a Life Estate pur autre vie (measured by the life of A)

B has an Indefeasibly Vested Remainder in Fee Simple Absolute

15. **O conveys Blackacre to A for ten years, then to the person who is then host of The Tonight Show.**

A has a Term of Years

The host of the Tonight Show has a Contingent Remainder in Fee Simple Absolute

O has a Reversion in Fee Simple Absolute

16. **O conveys Blackacre to A for ten years, then to B and his heirs if B gets married before A's estate ends.**

A has a Term of Years

B has a Contingent Remainder in Fee Simple Absolute

O has a Reversion in Fee Simple Absolute

17. O conveys Blackacre to A for life, then to B and her heirs, but if B does not survive A, then to C.

A has a Life Estate

B has a Vested Remainder Subject to Divestment in Fee Simple Absolute

C has a Shifting Executory Interest in Fee Simple Absolute

O has nothing.

18. O conveys Blackacre "to A for life, remainder to B if B survives A, but if not, to C and her heirs."

A has a Life Estate

B has a Contingent Remainder in Fee Simple Absolute

C has a Contingent Remainder in Fee Simple Absolute

19. O conveys Blackacre to A for life, then to B and her heirs for so long as B remains unmarried, then to C and her heirs.

A has a Life Estate

B has a Contingent Remainder in Fee Simple Subject to Executory Limitation

C has a Contingent Remainder in Fee Simple Absolute and a Shifting Executory Interest in Fee Simple Absolute

20. O conveys Blackacre to A for life, then to B and her heirs if B graduates from law school before A dies, but if B fails to graduate from law school before A dies, then to C and his heirs.

A has a Life Estate

B has a Contingent Remainder in Fee Simple Absolute

C has a Contingent Remainder in Fee Simple Absolute

CHAPTER 18

PROBLEM SET II: DEFEASIBLE FEES

ANSWERS FOR PRESENT ESTATES ONLY

1. O conveys Blackacre to A and her heirs so long as Blackacre is used for educational purposes.

A has a Fee Simple Determinable

2. O conveys Blackacre to A and her heirs, but if Blackacre is no longer used for educational purposes, then O has the right to reclaim Blackacre.

A has a Fee Simple Subject to Condition Subsequent

3. O conveys Blackacre to A and her heirs so long as Blackacre continues to be used for agricultural purposes, then to B and her heirs.

A has a Fee Simple Subject to Executory Limitation

4. O conveys Blackacre to A and her heirs, but if Blackacre is used for commercial purposes, then to B and her heirs.

A has a Fee Simple Subject to Executory Limitation

5. O conveys Blackacre to A and her heirs, unless Blackacre is used for commercial purposes.

A has a Fee Simple Subject to Condition Subsequent

6. O conveys Blackacre to A provided that he graduates from college before taking possession.

O has a Fee Simple Subject to Executory Limitation

7. O conveys Blackacre to A for life, then to B and her heirs so long as Blackacre continues to be farmed organically.

A has a Life Estate

B has an Indefeasibly Vested Remainder in Fee Simple Determinable

8. O conveys Blackacre to A for life, then to B and her heirs, but if Blackacre is used for commercial purposes following A's life estate, then to C and her heirs.

A has a Life Estate

B has an Indefeasibly Vested Remainder in Fee Simple Subject to Executory Limitation

9. O conveys Blackacre to A and her heirs until B graduates from college, then to B and her heirs.

A has a Fee Simple Subject to Executory Limitation

10. O devises to A and her heirs while the property is used for charitable purposes.

A has a Fee Simple Subject to Executory Limitation

11. O conveys Blackacre to A and his heirs, but if A allows liquor to be sold on Blackacre, to B if B is then living, and if B is not then living, to C and his heirs.

A has a Fee Simple Subject to Executory Limitation

12. O conveys Blackacre "to A and her heirs, on the express condition that Blackacre be used only for residential purposes."

A has a Fee Simple Subject to Condition Subsequent

13. O conveys Blackacre "to A and her heirs, it being my wish that Blackacre be used only for residential purposes."

A has a Fee Simple Absolute

14. O conveys Blackacre "to A, provided that the estate hereby granted to A shall automatically terminate if liquor is sold, used, or stored on the premises."

A has a Fee Simple Subject to Condition Subsequent

15. O devises Blackacre "to A, for so long as A continues to live on Blackacre."

A has a Life Estate Subject to Executory Limitation

CHAPTER 19
PROBLEM SET II: DEFEASIBLE FEES
COMPLETE ANSWERS

1. O conveys Blackacre to A and her heirs so long as Blackacre is used for educational purposes.

A has a Fee Simple Determinable

O has a Possibility of Reverter in Fee Simple Absolute

2. O conveys Blackacre to A and her heirs, but if Blackacre is no longer used for educational purposes, then O has the right to reclaim Blackacre.

A has a Fee Simple Subject to Condition Subsequent

O has a Right of Entry in Fee Simple Absolute

3. O conveys Blackacre to A and her heirs so long as Blackacre continues to be used for agricultural purposes, then to B and her heirs.

A has a Fee Simple Subject to Executory Limitation

B has a Shifting Executory Interest in Fee Simple Absolute

O has Nothing

4. O conveys Blackacre to A and her heirs, but if Blackacre is used for commercial purposes, then to B and her heirs.

A has a Fee Simple Subject to Executory Limitation

B has a Shifting Executory Interest in Fee Simple Absolute

5. O conveys Blackacre to A and her heirs, unless Blackacre is used for commercial purposes.

A has a Fee Simple Subject to Condition Subsequent

O has a Right of Entry in Fee Simple Absolute

6. **O conveys Blackacre to A provided that he graduates from college before taking possession.**

O has a Fee Simple Subject to Executory Limitation

A has a Springing Executory Interest in Fee Simple Absolute

7. **O conveys Blackacre to A for life, then to B and her heirs so long as Blackacre continues to be farmed organically.**

A has a Life Estate

B has an Indefeasibly Vested Remainder in Fee Simple Determinable

O has a Possibility of Reverter in Fee Simple Absolute

8. **O conveys Blackacre to A for life, then to B and her heirs, but if Blackacre is used for commercial purposes following A's life estate, then to C and her heirs.**

A has a Life Estate

B has an Indefeasibly Vested Remainder in Fee Simple Subject to Executory Limitation

C has a Shifting Executory Interest in Fee Simple Absolute

9. **O conveys Blackacre to A and her heirs until B graduates from college, then to B and her heirs.**

A has a Fee Simple Subject to Executory Limitation

B has a Shifting Executory Interest in Fee Simple Absolute

10. **O devises to A and her heirs while the property is used for charitable purposes.**

A has a Fee Simple Subject to Executory Limitation

O's Estate has a Shifting Executory Interest in Fee Simple Absolute

11. **O conveys Blackacre to A and his heirs, but if A allows liquor to be sold on Blackacre, to B if B is then living, and if B is not then living, to C and his heirs.**

A has a Fee Simple Subject to Executory Limitation

B has a Shifting Executory Interest in Fee Simple Absolute

C has a Shifting Executory Interest in Fee Simple Absolute

12. O conveys Blackacre "to A and her heirs, on the express condition that Blackacre be used only for residential purposes."

A has a Fee Simple Subject to Condition Subsequent

O has a Right of Entry in Fee Simple Absolute

13. O conveys Blackacre "to A and her heirs, it being my wish that Blackacre be used only for residential purposes."

A has a Fee Simple Absolute

14. O conveys Blackacre "to A, provided that the estate hereby granted to A shall automatically terminate if liquor is sold, used, or stored on the premises."

A has a Fee Simple Subject to Condition Subsequent

O has a Right of Entry in Fee Simple Absolute

15. O devises Blackacre "to A, for so long as A continues to live on Blackacre."

A has a Life Estate Subject to Executory Limitation

O's Estate has a Shifting Executory Interest

CHAPTER 20

PROBLEM SET III: REMAINDERS

COMPLETE ANSWERS

1. O conveys Blackacre to A for life, then if B is still living, to B and her heirs, but if B predeceases A, then to C and her heirs.

A has a Life Estate.

B has a Contingent Remainder in Fee Simple Absolute.

C has a Contingent Remainder in Fee Simple Absolute.

O has nothing.

2. O conveys Blackacre to A for life, then to B and his heirs if B goes straight from high school to college before A's death, and if B fails to do so, to C and her heirs.

A has a Life Estate.

B has a Contingent Remainder in Fee Simple Absolute.

C has a Contingent Remainder in Fee Simple Absolute.

O has nothing.

3. O conveys Blackacre to A for life, then to A's children and their heirs. At the time of the conveyance, A has one child, X.

A has a Life Estate.

X has a Vested Remainder Subject to Open in Fee Simple Absolute.

A's Unborn Children have a Contingent Remainder in Fee Simple Absolute.

O has nothing.

4. O conveys Blackacre to A for life, then to B.

A has a Life Estate.

B has an Indefeasibly Vested Remainder in Fee Simple Absolute.

O has nothing.

5. **O conveys Blackacre to A for life, then to B and his heirs if B lives to the age of 30. (Assume that B is currently age 25.)**

A has a Life Estate.

B has a Contingent Remainder in Fee Simple Absolute and a Springing Executory Interest in Fee Simple Absolute.

O has a Reversion in Fee Simple Subject to Executory Limitation

Explanation: There are three possibilities with this condition precedent: (1) B could turn 30 before A's death, (2) B could die before turning 30 (before A's death), or (3) B could be alive but not yet 30 at the time of A's death. In the event of (1), B's Contingent Remainder would convert to an Indefeasibly Vested Remainder and O's interests would terminate. In the event of (2), B's interest would terminate and O's interest would convert to a Reversion in Fee Simple Absolute. In the event of (3), Blackacre would revert back to O until B either turned 30 or died before turning 30. If B did then turn 30, Blackacre would go to B via a Springing Executory Interest in Fee Simple Absolute.

6. **O conveys Blackacre to A for life, then to B's children and their heirs. B has no children at the time of the conveyance.**

A has a Life Estate.

B's unborn children have a Contingent Remainder in Fee Simple Absolute.

O has a Reversion in Fee Simple Absolute.

7. **O devises Blackacre to A for life, then, if B survives A, to B, but if B does not survive A, then to C.**

A has a Life Estate.

B has a Contingent Remainder in Fee Simple Absolute.

C has a Contingent Remainder in Fee Simple Absolute.

O's Estate has Nothing.

8. O conveys Blackacre to A for life, then to B for life, then to C's children. Assume that C is alive at the time of the conveyance and has one child, M.

A has a Life Estate.

B has an Indefeasibly Vested Remainder in Life Estate.

C has nothing.

M has a Vested Remainder Subject to Open in Fee Simple Absolute.

C's unborn children have a Contingent Remainder in Fee Simple Absolute.

O has nothing.

9. O conveys Blackacre to A for ten years, then to the then-current Governor of North Carolina.

A has a Term of Years.

The then-current Governor of North Carolina has a Contingent Remainder in Fee Simple Absolute.

O has a Reversion in Fee Simple Absolute.

10. O devises Blackacre to A for life, then to B and his heirs if B gets married before A dies.

A has a Life Estate.

B has a Contingent Remainder in Fee Simple Absolute.

O's Estate has a Contingent Remainder in Fee Simple Absolute.

11. O conveys Blackacre to A for life, then to B and her heirs as long as Blackacre continues to be farmed organically.

A has a Life Estate.

B has an Indefeasibly Vested Remainder in Fee Simple Determinable.

O has a Possibility of Reverter in Fee Simple Absolute.

12. O devises Blackacre to A for life, then to B and his heirs if B survives A.

A has a Life Estate.

B has a Contingent Remainder in Fee Simple Absolute.

O's Estate has a Contingent Remainder in Fee Simple Absolute.

13. O conveys Blackacre to A for life, then to B for life, then to C and her heirs if C quits smoking before B dies.

A has a Life Estate.

B has an Indefeasibly Vested Remainder in Life Estate.

C has a Contingent Remainder in Fee Simple Absolute.

O has a Reversion in Fee Simple Absolute.

14. O devises Blackacre to A for two years, then to B for life, then to C and her heirs as long as Blackacre is used for charitable purposes, any remaining interest to D and his heirs.

A has a Term of Years.

B has an Indefeasibly Vested Remainder in Life Estate.

C has an Indefeasibly Vested Remainder in Fee Simple Subject to Executory Limitation.

D has a Shifting Executory Interest in Fee Simple Absolute.

O's Estate has nothing.

15. O conveys Blackacre "to A for life, then to return to me for life, then to C."

A has a Life Estate

O has a Reversion in Life Estate

C has an Indefeasibly Vested Remainder in Fee Simple Absolute

16. O conveys Blackacre to A for ten years, then to B for life, then to B's heirs.

A has a Term of Years

B has an Indefeasibly Vested Remainder in Life Estate

B's heirs have a Contingent Remainder in Fee Simple Absolute

O has a Reversion in Fee Simple Absolute

CHAPTER 21
PROBLEM SET IV: REVIEW
COMPLETE ANSWERS

1. **O conveys Blackacre to A.**

A has a Fee Simple Absolute.

O has nothing.

2. **O devises Blackacre to A.**

A has a Fee Simple Absolute.

O has nothing.

3. **O conveys Blackacre to A for life.**

A has a Life Estate.

O has a Reversion in Fee Simple Absolute.

4. **O devises Blackacre to A for life.**

A has a Life Estate.

O's Estate has an Indefeasibly Vested Remainder in Fee Simple Absolute.

5. **O conveys Blackacre to A for life, then to B.**

A has a Life Estate.

B has an Indefeasibly Vested Remainder in Fee Simple Absolute.

O has nothing.

6. **O conveys Blackacre to A and the heirs of her body.**

A has a Fee Tail.

O has a Reversion in Fee Simple Absolute.

7. **O devises Blackacre to A and the heirs of her body.**

A has a Fee Tail.

O's Estate has an Indefeasibly Vested Remainder in Fee Simple Absolute.

8. **O conveys Blackacre to A and the heirs of her body, then to B.**

A has a Fee Tail.

B has an Indefeasibly Vested Remainder in Fee Simple Absolute.

O has nothing.

9. **O conveys Blackacre to A for a period of two years.**

A has a Term of Years.

O has a Reversion in Fee Simple Absolute.

10. **O devises Blackacre to A for a period of two years.**

A has a Term of Years.

O's Estate has an Indefeasibly Vested Remainder in Fee Simple Absolute.

11. **O conveys Blackacre to A for a period of two years, then to B.**

A has a Term of Years.

B has an Indefeasibly Vested Remainder in Fee Simple Absolute.

O has nothing.

12. **O conveys Blackacre to A as long as Blackacre is used as a cat sanctuary.**

A has a Fee Simple Determinable.

O has a Possibility of Reverter in Fee Simple Absolute.

13. **O devises Blackacre to A as long as Blackacre is used as a cat sanctuary.**

A has a Fee Simple Subject to Executory Limitation.

O's Estate has a Shifting Executory Interest in Fee Simple Absolute.

14. O conveys Blackacre to A as long as Blackacre it used as a cat sanctuary, then to B.

A has a Fee Simple Subject to Executory Limitation.

B has a Shifting Executory Interest in Fee Simple Absolute.

O has nothing.

15. O conveys Blackacre to A, provided that dogs are not allowed on Blackacre.

A has a Fee Simple Subject to Condition Subsequent.

O has a Right of Entry in Fee Simple Absolute.

16. O devises Blackacre to A, provided that dogs are not allowed on Blackacre.

A has a Fee Simple Subject to Executory Limitation.

O's Estate has a Shifting Executory Interest in Fee Simple Absolute.

17. O conveys Blackacre to A, provided that dogs are not allowed on Blackacre, thereafter to B.

A has a Fee Simple Subject to Executory Limitation.

B has a Shifting Executory Interest in Fee Simple Absolute.

O has nothing.

18. O conveys Blackacre to A, provided that dogs are not allowed on Blackacre, and if dogs are allowed on Blackacre, B shall have the right to enter and take possession.

A has a Fee Simple Subject to Executory Limitation.

B has a Shifting Executory Interest in Fee Simple Absolute.

O has nothing.

19. O conveys Blackacre to A if and when A graduates from law school.

O has a Fee Simple Subject to Executory Limitation.

A has a Springing Executory Interest in Fee Simple Absolute.

20. O devises Blackacre to A if and when A graduates from law school.

O's Estate has a Fee Simple Subject to Executory Limitation.

A has a Shifting Executory Interest in Fee Simple Absolute.

21. O conveys Blackacre to A but if B graduates from law school, to B.

A has a Fee Simple Subject to Executory Limitation.

B has a Shifting Executory Interest in Fee Simple Absolute.

O has nothing.

22. O conveys Blackacre to A for life, then to B only if B promises to never, ever allow dogs on Blackacre.

A has a Life Estate.

B has a Contingent Remainder in Fee Simple Absolute.

O has a Reversion in Fee Simple Absolute.

23. O devises Blackacre to A for life, then to B only if B promises to never, ever allow dogs on Blackacre.

A has a Life Estate.

B has a Contingent Remainder in Fee Simple Absolute.

O's Estate has a Contingent Remainder in Fee Simple Absolute.

24. O conveys Blackacre to A for life, then to B only if B promises to never, ever allow dogs on Blackacre and then only so long as no dogs are allowed on Blackacre.

A has a Life Estate.

B has a Contingent Remainder in Fee Simple Determinable (there is both a condition precedent and a condition subsequent).

O has two interests:

- *a Reversion in Fee Simple Absolute (if B fails to promise); and*
- *a Possibility of Reverter in Fee Simple Absolute (if B does promise but later allows dogs on Blackacre.)*

25. O conveys Blackacre to A for life, then to B only if B promises to never, ever allow dogs on Blackacre and then only so long as no dogs are allowed on Blackacre, and if B fails to promise or if dogs are ever allowed on Blackacre, then to C.

A has a Life Estate.

B has a Contingent Remainder in Fee Simple Subject to Executory Limitation (there is both a condition precedent and a condition subsequent).

C has two interests:

- *A Contingent Remainder in Fee Simple Absolute (if B fails to promise); and*
- *A Shifting Executory Interest in Fee Simple Absolute (if B does promise but later allows dogs on Blackacre).*

O has nothing.

26. O conveys Blackacre to A for life, then to A's oldest living child at the time of A's death. A has three children at the time of the conveyance: X, Y, and Z.

A has a Life Estate.

A's oldest living child at the time of A's death has a Contingent Remainder in Fee Simple Absolute.

O has a Reversion in Fee Simple Absolute.

X, Y, and Z have nothing.

27. O devises Blackacre to A for life, then to A's oldest living child at the time of A's death. A has three children at the time of the conveyance: X, Y, and Z.

A has a Life Estate.

A's oldest living child at the time of A's death has a Contingent Remainder in Fee Simple Absolute.

O's Estate has a Contingent Remainder in Fee Simple Absolute.

X, Y, and Z have nothing.

28. O conveys Blackacre to A for life, then to A's then-living children. A has three children living at the time of the conveyance: X, Y, and Z.

A has a Life Estate.

X, Y, and Z each have a Contingent Remainder in Fee Simple Absolute.

O has a Reversion in Fee Simple Absolute.

29. **O devises Blackacre to A for life, then to A's then-living children. A has three children living at the time of the conveyance: X, Y, and Z.**

A has a Life Estate.

X, Y, and Z each have a Contingent Remainder in Fee Simple Absolute.

O's Estate has a Contingent Remainder in Fee Simple Absolute.

30. **O conveys Blackacre to A for life, then to A's children. A has three children living at the time of the conveyance: X, Y, and Z.**

A has a Life Estate.

X, Y, and Z each have a Vested Remainder Subject to Open in Fee Simple Absolute.

A's potential unborn children have a Contingent Remainder in Fee Simple Absolute.

O has nothing.

31. **O devises Blackacre to A for life, then to A's children. A has three children living at the time of the devise: X, Y, and Z.**

A has a Life Estate.

X, Y, and Z each have a Vested Remainder Subject to Open in Fee Simple Absolute.

A's potential unborn children have a Contingent Remainder in Fee Simple Absolute.

O's Estate has nothing.

32. **O conveys Blackacre to A for life, then to A's children for life, then to A's grandchildren. At the time of the conveyance, A has one child, X, and no grandchildren.**

A has a Life Estate.

X has a Vested Remainder Subject to Open in Life Estate.

A's potential unborn children have a Contingent Remainder in Life Estate.

A's potential unborn grandchildren have a Contingent Remainder in Fee Simple Absolute.

O has a Reversion in Fee Simple Absolute.

33. O conveys Blackacre to A for life, then to A's children for life, then to A's grandchildren. At the time of the conveyance, A has one child, X, and one grandchild, M.

A has a Life Estate.

X has a Vested Remainder Subject to Open in Life Estate.

A's potential unborn children have a Contingent Remainder in Life Estate.

M has a Vested Remainder Subject to Open in Fee Simple Absolute.

A's potential unborn grandchildren have a Contingent Remainder in Fee Simple Absolute.

O has nothing.

ABOUT THE AUTHOR

Tanya D. Marsh is a Professor at Wake Forest University School of Law in Winston-Salem, North Carolina, where she teaches Property, Decedents' Estates and Trusts, courses in real estate, and Funeral and Cemetery Law. Marsh is a graduate of Indiana University and Harvard Law School.

Made in the USA
Columbia, SC
27 August 2021